A Gift Book of

Love & Marriage

To

GRAHAM & ADA

with love from

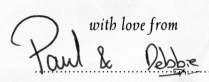

If thou must love me, let it not be for nought
Except for love's sake only. Do not say,
'I love her for her smile — her look — her way
Of speaking gently,— for a trick of thought
That falls in well with mine, and certes brought
A sense of pleasant ease on such a day' —
For these things in themselves, Beloved, may
Be changed, or change for thee and love, so wrought,
May be unwrought so. Neither love me for
Thine own dear pity's wiping my cheeks dry,—
A creature might forget to weep, who bore
Thy comfort long, and lose thy love thereby!
But love me for love's sake, that evermore
Thou mayest love on, through love's eternity.

Elizabeth Barrett Browning (1806–61)

A Gift Book of

Love & Marriage

by Deborah Nixon

WELDON
PUBLISHING

A Kevin Weldon Production

Published by Weldon Publishing
a division of Kevin Weldon & Associates Pty Limited
Level 5, 70 George Street, Sydney, NSW 2000, Australia

First published in 1992

© Copyright selection and design:
Kevin Weldon & Associates Pty Limited 1992
Designer: Catherine Martin
Photographer: Andrew Elton
Project Co-ordinator: Deborah Nixon
Printed in Hong Kong by South China Printing Company (1988) Limited

National Library of Australia Cataloguing-in-Publication data:

A Gift Book of Love and Marriage
ISBN 1 86302 234 1
1. Love – Literary collections. 2. Love poetry, English. 3. Marriage –
Literary collections. 4. English Literature. I. Nixon, Deborah.
820.80354

Contents

The Romance 6

The Question 14

The Decision 22

The Wedding 32

The Marriage 64

The Golden Years 72

The Romance

'How do I love thee?'

———

How do I love thee? Let me count the ways.
I love thee to the depth and breadth and height
My soul can reach, when feeling out of sight
For the ends of Being and ideal Grace.
I love thee to the level of every day's
Most quiet need, by sun and candle-light.
I love thee freely, as men strive for right;
I love thee purely, as they turn from praise.
I love thee with the passion put to use
In my old griefs, and with my childhood's faith.
I love thee with a love I seemed to lose
With my lost saints — I love thee with the breath,
Smiles, tears of all my life! — and if God choose
I shall but love thee better after death.

Elizabeth Barrett Browning (1806–61)

Shall I compare thee to a summer's day?
Thou art more lovely and more temperate:
Rough winds do shake the darling buds of May,
And summer's lease hath all too short a date:
Sometimes too hot the eye of heaven shines,
And often is his gold complexion dimm'd,
And every fair from fair sometimes declines,
By chance, or nature's changing course, untrim'd,
But thy eternal summer shall not fade,
Nor lose possession of that fair thou ow'st,
Nor shall death brag thou wandr'st in his shade,
When in eternal lines to time thou grow'st,
So long as men can breathe or eyes can see,
So long lives this, and this gives life to thee.

William Shakespeare (1564–1616)

I
LOVE
Thee

Elizabeth Bennett and Mr Darcy:

Elizabeth's spirits soon rising to playfulness again, she wanted Mr Darcy to account for his ever having fallen in love with her. 'How could you begin?' said she. 'I can comprehend your going on charmingly, when you had once made a beginning; but what could set you off in the first place?'

'I cannot fix on the hour, or the spot, or the look, or the words, which laid the foundation. It is too long ago. I was in the middle before I knew that I had begun.'

'My beauty you had early withstood, and as for my manners — my behaviour to you was at least always bordering on the uncivil, and I never spoke to you without rather wishing to give you pain than not. Now, be sincere; did you admire me for my impertinence?'

'For the liveliness of your mind, I did.'

'You may as well call it impertinence at once. It was very little less. The fact is, that you were sick of civility, of deference, of officious attention. You were disgusted with the women who were always speaking and looking and thinking for your approbation alone. I roused and interested you, because I was so unlike them. Had you not really been amiable, you would have hated me for it; but in spite of the pains you took to disguise yourself, your feelings were always noble and just; and, in your heart, you thoroughly despised the persons who so assiduously courted you. There— I have saved you the trouble of accounting for it; and really all things considered, I begin to think it perfectly reasonable. To be sure, you know no actual good of me — but nobody thinks of that when they fall in love.'

Jane Austen (1775–1817),
Pride and Prejudice

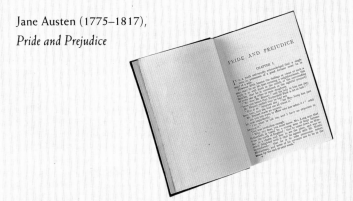

ℒove is soft and love is sweet, and speaks in accents fair;
Love is mighty agony, and love is mighty care;
Love is utmost ecstasy and love is keen to dare:
Love is wretched misery; to live with, it's despair.

Wild Nights – Wild Nights!
Were I with thee
Wild Nights should be
Our luxury!

Futile – the Winds –
To a heart in port –
Done with the Compass –
Done with the Chart!

Rowing in Eden –
Ah! The Sea!
Might I but moor– Tonight –
In Thee!

Emily Dickinson (1830–86)

An Overwashed Moon.

13

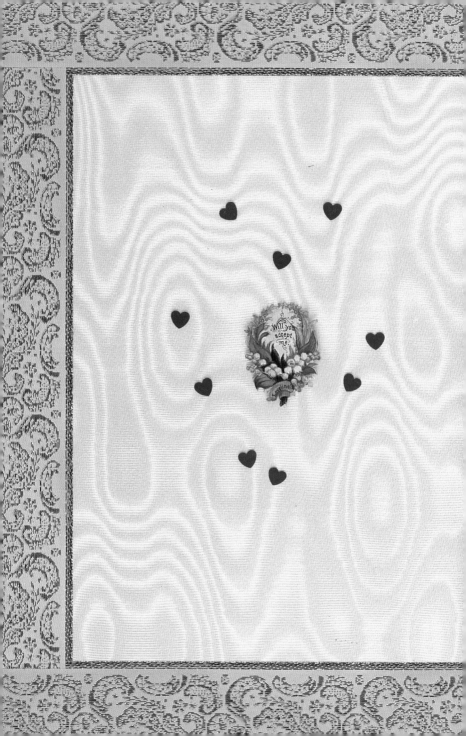

The Question

'Will thou have me?'

This is the Question
Marry   Not Marry

Charles Darwin

Come live with me and be my Love,
And we will all the pleasures prove
That hills and valleys, dales and fields,
Or woods or sleepy mountain yields.
And we will sit upon the rocks,
And see the shepherds feed their flocks
By shallow rivers, to whose falls
Melodious birds sing madrigals.
And I will make thee beds of roses
And a thousand fragrant posies;
A cap of flowers, and a kirtle
Embroidered all with leaves of myrtle.
A gown made of the finest wool
Which from our pretty lambs we pull;
Fair-lined slippers for the cold,
With buckles of the purest gold.
A belt of straw and ivy-buds
With coral clasps and amber studs:
And if these pleasures may thee move,
Come live with me and be my Love.
The shepherd swains shall dance and sing
For thy delight each May morning:
If these delights thy mind may move;
Then live with me and be my Love.

Christopher Marlowe (1564–93)

At what age is it best for a man to marry?
In youth it is too soon, and in age it is too late.

Diogenes (412–323 BC)

Mr Rochester to Jane Eyre:

After a youth and manhood passed half in unutterable misery and half in dreary solitude, I have for the first time found what I can truly love – I have found you. You are my sympathy – my better half – my good angel – I am bound to you with a strong attachment. I think you good, gifted, lovely: a fervent, solemn passion is conceived in my heart: it leans to you, draws you to my centre and spring of life, wraps my existence about you – and, kindling in pure powerful flame, fuses you and me in one.

It was because I felt and knew this, that I resolved to marry you. To tell me that I had already a wife is empty mockery: you know now that I had but a hideous demon. I was wrong to attempt to deceive you; but I feared a stubborness that exists in your character. I feared early instilled prejudice: I wanted to have you safe before hazarding confidences. This was cowardly: I should have appealed to your nobleness and magnanimity at first, as I do now, opened to you my life of agony – described to you my hunger and thirst after a higher and worthier existence – shown to you, not my resolution (that word is weak), but my resistless bent to love faithfully and well, where I am faithfully and well loved in return. Then I should have asked you to accept my pledge of fidelity, and to give me yours: Jane – give me it now.

Charlotte Brontë (1816–55), *Jane Eyre*

$\mathcal{Q}$oth John to Joan, will thou have me:
I prithee now, wilt? and I'll marry thee
My cow, my calf, my house, my rents,
And all my lands and tenements:
    Oh, say, my Joan, will not that do?
    I cannot come every day to woo.

Anon.

$\mathcal{S}$omeone has said that there would be fewer divorces if more proposals were made in the middle of the day under ordinary conditions, but in any case the proposal itself should be made in sincere and earnest language ... often the more simple the proposal the more forcibly it expresses the suitor's feelings.

Lady Troubridge, *Book of Etiquette*, 1913

*A*dvice to a young man seeking a wife:

1. Mind where you pick her up.
2. Select the daughter of a good mother.
3. See that she is of domestic habits.
4. Seek one that knows the worth of money.
5. Seek a person of suitable temperament.
6. Seek a person of sound character.
7. Seek a person of good health.
8. Seek a person of religious character.

*A*dvice to a young woman seeking a husband:

1. Know something about him.
2. See that he is respectable.
3. See that he is careful and provident.
4. See that he is industrious.
5. See that he is of good moral character.
6. See that he is honest.
7. He should have a good temper.
8. He should have good health.
9. He should be religious in his life.

Job Flower, *Golden Guide to Matrimony*, 1882

21

The Decision

'No wandering any more.'

—

'You Jane. I must have you for my own entirely my own. Will you be mine? Say yes, quickly.'

'Mr Rochester, let me look at your face: turn to the moonlight.'

'Why?'

'Because I want to read your countenance; turn!'

'There you will find it scarcely more legible than a crumpled, scratched page. Read on: only make haste, for I suffer.'

His face was very much agitated and very much flushed, and there were strong workings in his features, and strange gleams in the eyes.

'Oh, Jane, you torture me!' he exclaimed. 'With that searching and yet faithful and generous look, you torture me!'

'How can I do that? If you are true and your offer real, my only feelings to you must be gratitude and devotion— they cannot torture.'

'Gratitude!' he ejaculated; and added wildly —'Jane, accept me quickly. Say Edward— give me my name — Edward — I will marry you.'

'Are you in earnest?— do you truly love me? —Do you sincerely wish me to be your wife?'

'I do; and if an oath is neccessary to satisfy you, I swear it.'

'Then, sir, I will marry you.'

Charlotte Brontë (1816–55), *Jane Eyre*

*C*atherine Arrowpoint and Herr Klesmer:

'*Why should I not marry the man who loves me, if I love him?*' said Catherine. To her the effort was something like the leap of a woman from the deck into the lifeboat.

'*It would be too hard — impossible— you could not carry it through. I am not worth what you would have to encounter. I will not accept the sacrifice. It would be thought a Mesalliance for you, and I should be liable to the worst accusations.*'

'*Is it the accusations you are afraid of? I am afraid of nothing but that we should miss the passing of our lives together.*'

The decisive word had been spoken: there was no doubt concerning the end willed by each: there only remained the way of arriving at it, and Catherine determined to take the straightest possible. She went to her father and mother in the library, and told them that she had promised to marry Klesmer.

George Eliot (1819–80), *Daniel Deronda*

Miranda: *Do you love me?*

Ferdinand: *O heaven, O earth,*
bear witness to this sound,
And crown what I profess with kind event
If I speak true! if hollowly, invert
What best is boded me to mischief! I,
Beyond all limit of what else i' the world,
Do love, prize, honour you.

Miranda: *I am a fool*
To weep at what I am glad of.

Prospero: *Fair encounter*
Of two most rare affections! Heavens rain grace
On that which breeds between'em!

Ferdinand: *Wherefore weep you?*

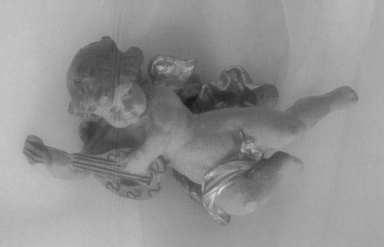

Miranda: *At mine unworthiness, that dare not offer*
What I desire to give; and much less take
What I shall die to want. But this is trifling;
And all the more it seeks to hide itself
The bigger bulk it shows. Hence, bashful cunning!
And prompt me, plain and holy innocence!
I am your wife, if you will marry me;
If not, I'll die your maid; to be your servant,
Whether you will or no.

Ferdinand: *My mistress, dearest;*
And I thus humble ever;

Miranda: *My husband, then?*

Ferdinand: *Ay, with a heart as willing*
As bondage e'er of freedom: here's my hand.

Miranda: *And mine, with my heart in't: and now farewell*
Till half an hour hence.

William Shakespeare (1564–1616), *The Tempest*

No wandering any more where the feet may stumble
Upon a sudden rise, or sink in damp
Marsh grasses. No uncertain following on
With nothing there to follow — a sure bird,
A fence, a farmhouse. No adventuring now
Where motion that is yet not motion dies.
Circles have lost their magic, and the voice
Comes back upon itself ... The road is firm.

It runs, and the dust is not too deep, and the end
Never can heave in sight — though one is there.
It runs in a straight silence, til a word
Turns it; then a sentence, and evening falls
At an expected inn, whose barest room
Cannot be lonely if a hand is reached
To touch another hand, the walls forgotten ...
Laughter is morning, and the road resumes;
Adventurous, it never will return.

Mark Van Doren, 'Marriage'

After a proposal of matrimony has been accepted it has long been tradition to give a ring as part of the covenant of the engagement. Solitaire diamond rings are a mark of the modern engagement. In the 18th and 19th centuries, various precious stones were set in the engagement ring so as to spell out with their initial letters special words such as LOVE or DEAREST or the betrothed's name (PEARL– Pearl, Emerald, Amethyst, Ruby, Lapis-Lazuli).

In France they are known as 'regard' rings and the gemstones form that word (Ruby, Emerald, Garnet, Amethyst, Ruby, Diamond). The significance of the stones varies from country to country, but common meanings are:

January	garnet
February	amethyst
March	bloodstone
April	diamond
May	emerald
June	pearl
July	ruby
August	sardonyx
September	sapphire
October	opal
November	topaz
December	turquoise

Precious stones have their virtues:

Turquoise: harmony
Emerald: success in love
Diamond: innocence and light
Ruby: chastity
Sardonyx: happiness
Topaz: fidelity
Amethyst: sincerity
Bloodstone: courage
Garnet: truth and constancy

The Wedding

'To the nuptial bowre.'

———

As are those dulcet sounds in the break of day
That creep into the dreaming bridegrooms ear
And summon him to marriage.

William Shakespeare, *The Merchant of Venice*

The sun-beames in the East are spred,
Leave, leave, faire Bride, your solitary bed,
No more shall you returne to it alone,
It nourseth sadnesse, and your bodies print,
Like to a grave, the yeilding down doth dint:
You and your other you meet there anon;
Put forth, put forth that warme balm-breathing thigh,
Which when next time you in these sheets will smother,
There it must meet another.
Come glad from thence, goe gladder than you came,
Today put on perfection and a woman's name.

John Donne (1572–1631), *'Epithalamion made at Lincoln's Inn'*

Open the temple gates unto my love,
Open them wide that she may enter in,
And all the postes adorne as doct behove,
And all the pillours deck with girlands trim,
For to recyve this Saynt with honour dew,
That commeth in to you...
Behold whiles she before the alter stands
Hearing the holy priest that to her speakes
And blesseth her with his two happy hands,
How the red roses flush up in her cheekes,
And the pure snow with goodly vermill stayne,
Like crimson dyed in grayne,
That even th'Angels which continually,
About the Altare doe remaine,
Forget their service and about her fly;
Ofte peeping in her face that seems more fayre,
The more they on it stare....
Sing ye sweet Angels, Alleluya sing,
That all the woods answere and your eccho ring.

Edmund Spenser (1552–99), from 'Epithalamion'

*There are not many men who lie abed too late
or oversleep themselves on their wedding morning.*

Charles Dickens

*If you love I as I love you,
No knife shall cut our love in two.*

To the Nuptial Bowre
I led her blushing like the Morn: all Heav'n
And happie Constellations on that houre
Shed their selectest influence; the Earth
Gave sign of gratulation, and each Hill;
Joyous the Birds: fresh Gales and gentle Aires
Whisper'd it to the Woods, and from thir wings
Flung Rose, flung Odours from the spicie Shrub,
Disporting, till the amorous Bird of Night
Sung Spousal, and bid haste the Eevning Starr
On his Hill top, to light the bridal Lamp.

John Milton (1608–74), *Paradise Lost*

What need of clamorous bells, or ribands gay,
These humble nuptials to proclaim or grace?
Angels of love, look down upon the place;
Shed on the chosen vale a sun-bright day!
Yet no proud gladness would the bride display
Even for such a promise: — serious is her face,
Modest her mien; and she whose thoughts keep pace
With gentleness, in that becoming way
Will thank you. Faultless does the maid appear,
No disproportion in her soul, no strife:
But, when the closer view of wedded life
Hath shown that nothing human can be clear
From frailty, for that insight may the Wife
To the indulgent Lord become more dear.

William Wordsworth (1770–1850)

Hear the mellow wedding bells, —
Golden bells
What a world of happiness their harmony foretells!
Through the balmy air of night
How they ring out their delight!
From the molten golden notes,
What a liquid ditty floats
To the turtle-dove that listens, while she gloats
On the moon!
Oh, from out the sounding cells,
What a gush of euphony voluminously wells!
How it swells!
How it dwells

On the future! How it tells
Of the rapture that impels
To the swinging and the ringing
Of the bells, bells, bells,
Of the bells, bells, bells, bells,
Bells, bells, bells, —
To the rhyming and the chiming of the bells!

Edgar Allan Poe (1809–49), from 'The Bells'

The Bridal Bouquet

The origin of the bridal bouquet goes back to ancient Rome where the bride carried ears of wheat or corn to ensure that her new husband's grain supplies would always be plentiful. By the 15th century the wheat stalks became a sheaf and by the 18th century carrying a bouquet of flowers became customary, a practice followed to this day. Individual flowers have particular meanings, but in general the flower bouquet is a symbol of happiness and good luck.

To a Bride

When thy foot is at the altar,
When the ring hath press'd thy hand,
When those thou lov'st, and those who love thee,
Smiling round thee stand,
O, may the verse that friendship weaves,
Like a spirit of the air,
Be o'er thee at that moment,
For a blessing and a prayer.

Anon.

In the language of flowers
the bride may wish to send a
message to her future husband:

Baby's breath: fertility
Daisy: innocence
Honeysuckle: happiness
Ivy: fertility and friendship
Jonquils: affection
Lilac: first love
Orange blossom: purity
Pink azalias: temperance
Pink roses: happy love
Red chrysanthemums: I love you

Red pinks: pure and ardent love
Red roses: love and romance
Red and white roses: unity
Rosemary: remembrance
Violets: faithfulness
Wattle: sensitivity
White heather: good fortune
White roses: purity
White stock: lasting beauty

Fair weather weddings make fair weather lives.

Richard Hovey, *The Marriage of Guenevere*

There is much folklore about the best time to marry and brides in the past took great care when choosing the month and day. June has long been the favoured month for weddings in the northern hemisphere. The brides of ancient Rome preferred the month of June as Juno was the goddess who took care of love matters and feminine interests. Wednesday may have once been 'the best day of all' but its popularity has declined in recent years.

Marry when the year is new,
Always loving, kind and true.
When February birds do mate,
You may wed, nor dread your fate.
If you wed when March winds blow,
Joy and sorrow both you'll know.
Marry in April when you can,
Joy for maiden and for man.
Marry in the month of May,
You will surely rue the day.
Marry when June roses blow,
Over sea and land you'll go.

They who in July do wed,
Must labour always for their bread.
Whoever wed in August be,
Many a change are sure to see.
Marry in September's shine,
Your living will be fair and fine.
If in October you do marry,
Love will come, but riches tarry.
If you wed in bleak November,
Only joy will come, remember.
When December's snows fall fast,
Marry, and true love will last.

Monday for wealth,
Tuesday for health,
Wednesday the best day of all,
Thursday for losses,
Friday for crosses,
And Saturday no luck at all.

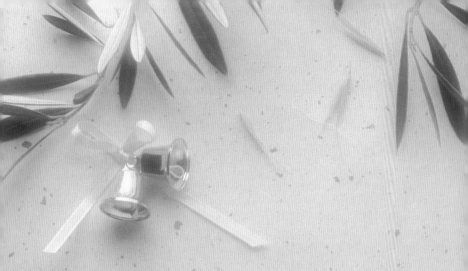

The Cid's Wedding

It was the glad espousals, with joy and wild uproar,
The streets were filled with people, and from balcony and floor
Beamed forth ten thousand faces that wore a general smile,
And buzz of voices, tread of feet, rose everywhere meanwhile.
Lain Calvo, the Lord Bishop, came first on ambling mule:
And close behind him, at his heels, rode fast the motley fool,
With cap and bell and bladder, upon a capering ass,
And the people tossed and shouted and laughed to see him pass.
Through rush-strewn street and jostling crowd did the long procession march,
Where lance and shield and helm and lance made many a glittering arch;
And olive branches, gay festoones, from house to house were spread,
And flags, that from the windows flung, flapped grandly overhead.
From crowds of hands flew showers of wheat, till the very air grew dark;
And every shooter, young and old, made the shrinking bride his mark;
And from her shoulders and her breast, wherever it had lain,
The wily king, with meaning look, picked off the scattered grain.
Then laughed the fool with sudden voice that all might understand;
"Tis well to be the king, I trow; but I had rather be that hand."

The white wedding is a tradition of the 20th century. In earlier times the bride merely wore her best dress and the colour she chose was believed to colour her future life:

> Married in white, you have chosen all right
> Married in blue, you will always be true
> Married in yellow, ashamed of your fellow
> Married in red, you wish yourself dead
> Married in black, you will wish yourself back
> Married in grey, you'll go far away
> Married in pink, your fortunes will sink
> Married in green, ashamed to be seen.

The significance of the different colours varies from country to country. Red is the nuptial colour in China, where it is said to represent wedding happiness. In Norway, green in a wedding outfit is perfectly acceptable, and in Orthodox Jewish weddings the bridegroom also wears white.

Many superstitions surround the wedding dress. It was believed that a hair sewn into the dress acted as a good luck charm and a sprinkling of sugar into the hem ensured sweetness throughout married life while a coin sewn into the seams would bring prosperity. Black thread was never used as it was thought to bring bad luck.

Blest is the bride on whom the sun does shine.

Robert Herrick, 'A Nuptial Song'

A Marriage Ring

The ring so worn as you behold,
So thin, so pale, is yet of gold:
The passion such it was to prove:
Worn with life's cares, love yet was love.

George Crabbe, 1754–1832

The ring is on my hand,
And the wreath is on my brow;
Satins and jewels grand
Are all at my command,
And I am happy now.

Edgar Allan Poe (1809–49),
'Bridal Ballad'

Go little ring to that same sweet
That hath my heart in her domain. . .

Geoffrey Chaucer (1340–1400)

Loose though it be,
The joint is free;
So, when love's yoke is on,
It must not gall,
Nor fret at all,
With hard oppression.

But it must play,
Still either way,
And be, too, such a yoke
As not too wide
To overslide,
Or be so straight to choke.

So we who bear
This beam, must rear
Ourselves to such a height
As that the stay
Of either may
Create the burthen light.

And as this round
Is nowhere found
To flaw, or else to sever,
So let our love
As endless prove,
And pure as gold forever.

Robert Herrick (1868–1938),
'A ring presented to Julia'

The Wedding Cake

The cutting of the cake is one of the oldest nuptial rites dating back to Roman times where the breaking of cake symbolised fertility and abundance. In the early 18th century the custom was to break the cake over the bride's head; the pieces would then be given to her friends to eat so that they would see a vision of the person destined to be their future wife or husband. A variation on this was to draw a thin slice of cake through the wedding ring and the lucky recipients would place the cake under their pillows to dream of their future loved one. Another tradition has it that if a plate of crumbs is thrown out the window the shattered pieces represent good luck. The more pieces, the better the luck.

Nowadays, pieces of the wedding cake are wrapped in paper or small boxes and distributed to the guests.

But, madam, as a present take,
This little paper of bride-cake;
Fast any Friday in the year,
When Venus mounts the starry sphere,
Thrust this at night in pillow beer;
In morning slumber you will seem
T'enjoy your lover in a dream.

c. 1733

*T*he table was laid in the cart-shed. On it were four sirloins, six frickasees of chicken, stewed veal, three legs of mutton, and in the middle a fine roast of suckling pig, flanked by four chitterlings with sorrel. At the corners were decanters of brandy. Sweet cider frothed round the corks of the bottles, and all the glasses had already been filled to the brim with wine. Large dishes of yellow cream, that trembled with the least shake of the table, had the initials of the newly wedded pair drawn in nonpareil arabesques on their smooth surface. A confectioner from Yvetot had been entrusted with the tarts and sweets. As he had only just set up in business, he had taken a lot of trouble and at dessert he himself brought in a set dish that evoked loud cries of wonderment. Starting at the base there

was a square of blue cardboard, representing a temple, with porticoes, colonnades and stucco statuettes all round, and constellations of gilt paper stars in the niches; then on the second stage was a dungeon keep of Savoy cake, surrounded by tiny fortifications made from candied angelica, almonds, raisins, and quarters of oranges; and finally, on the upper platform there was a green field with rocks set in lakes of jam, nutshell boats, and a small Cupid balanced on a chocolate swing with two uprights that ended in real roses instead of balls at the top.

Gustave Flaubert,
from *Madame Bovary*, 1856

The smallest piece of silver which can qualify as a wedding gift is a marmalade spoon.

Charles W. Morton

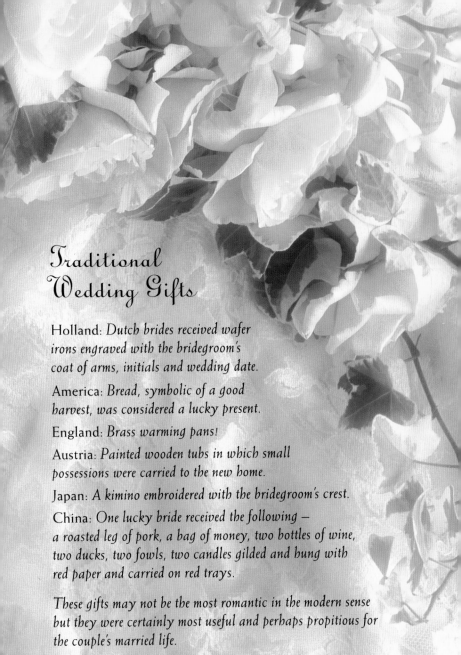

Traditional Wedding Gifts

Holland: *Dutch brides received wafer irons engraved with the bridegroom's coat of arms, initials and wedding date.*

America: *Bread, symbolic of a good harvest, was considered a lucky present.*

England: *Brass warming pans!*

Austria: *Painted wooden tubs in which small possessions were carried to the new home.*

Japan: *A kimino embroidered with the bridegroom's crest.*

China: *One lucky bride received the following — a roasted leg of pork, a bag of money, two bottles of wine, two ducks, two fowls, two candles gilded and hung with red paper and carried on red trays.*

These gifts may not be the most romantic in the modern sense but they were certainly most useful and perhaps propitious for the couple's married life.

Wedding traditions and customs

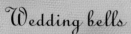

Wedding bells

Said to ward off evil spirits (noise intimidating the spirit world), the tolling of the bells also serves to announce that a wedding is under way.

The horseshoe

A symbol of good luck for centuries, the horseshoe should always be carried with the ends pointing up — to prevent the luck falling out.

The garter

The tradition of throwing the garter is a refined development of the old Anglo-Saxon custom of 'flying the stocking'.
During the ritual of 'bedding the bride' the men present would take the bride's stockings and the women would remove those of the bridegroom. They would then throw the stockings over their heads and the lucky person on whose head a stocking fell would be the next to marry. Tossing the bride's bouquet to the wedding guests is a modern variation on this theme.
In the 18th century the bride's garter was sometimes decorated with the couple's zodiacal signs.
Owning a garter worn by a bride and then having it back after the wedding is supposed to bring luck to the lender.

The veil

A bride wearing a veil over her face follows the custom dating from the days of marriage by purchase when the groom did not look at the bride until after the ceremony.

Wedding traditions and customs

Other superstitions and beliefs

Tradition has it that if a bride wants to avoid being dominated by her husband she must step out of the church with her left foot first. A related item of wedding lore is that whoever stomps on the other's foot first will be the dominating partner.

The old custom of giving the bride a blow on the head (gently, one hopes!) with a shoe given to the bridegroom by the bride's father to symbolise the passing over of authority has, happily, not survived.

Something old, something new,
Something borrowed, something blue.

Many modern brides try to follow this litany of wedding folklore to ensure good luck in their married life. The something old signifies a bride's link to her family and the past, something new represents the start of her new life, something borrowed represents the couple's link to family and friends and the something blue symbolises faithfulness, loyalty and constancy.

Throwing rice, confetti and flower petals

Throwing rice, confetti or flower petals over the newly married couple is a development of the ancient custom of throwing cake crumbs or grain over the bride and groom. This practice originally symbolised the hope for fertility in marriage. Today the rice, confetti or flower petals represent a more general wish for happiness and prosperity.

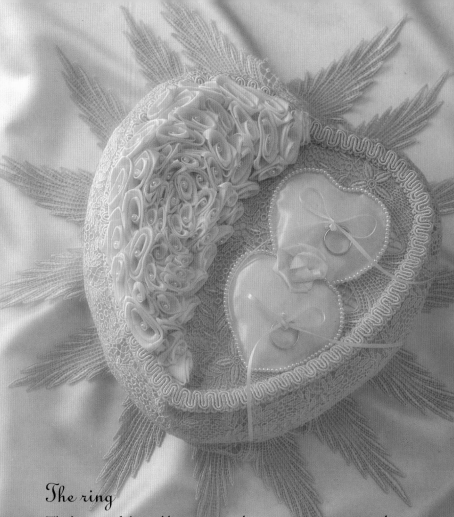

The ring

The history of the wedding ring is rich in poetic associations and lore. The custom of wearing the wedding ring on the third finger of the left hand comes from the belief that a vein or nerve ran direct from this finger to the heart. It has also been said that the ring is worn on this finger as it is the finger that is the least used.

The Egyptians were the first to use gold in wedding rings — the unbroken circle of the ring sybolised eternity and the perpetuity of matrimony.

The Marriage

'Stand together yet not too near.'

$\mathcal{M}$arriage is terrifying,
but so is a cold and forlorn old age.

Robert Louis Stevenson (1850–94)

$\mathcal{N}$otwithstanding all that wit, or malice, or pride,
or prudence will be able to suggest, men and women
must at last pass their lives together.

Dr Samuel Johnson (1709–84)

$\mathcal{L}$ike everything which is not the involuntary result of fleeing
emotion, but the creation of time and will, any marriage, happy
or unhappy, is infinitely more interesting and significant than
any romance, however passionate.

W.H. Auden (1907–73)

*Love one another, but make not
a bond of love:
Let it rather be a moving sea between the
shores of your souls.
Fill each other's cup but drink not from one cup.
Give one another of your bread but eat not from
the same loaf.
Sing and dance together and be joyous, but let
each of you be alone,
Even as strings of a lute are alone though they
quiver with the same music.
Give your hearts, but not into each other's keeping.
For only the hand of Life can contain your hearts.
And stand together yet not too near together:
For the pillars of the temple stand apart,
And the oak tree and the cypress grow not in
each other's shadow.*

Kahlil Gibran, *The Prophet*, 1923

Let me not to the marriage of true minds
Admit impediments. Love is not love
Which alters when it alteration finds,
Or bends with the remover to remove;
O, no! it is an ever-fixed mark,
That looks on tempests and is never shaken;
It is the star to every wandering bark,
Whose worth's unknown, although his height be taken.
Love's not time's fool, though rosy lips and cheeks
Within his bending sickle's compass come;
Love alters not with his brief hours and weeks,
But bears it out even to the edge of doom.
    If this is error, and upon me prov'd,
    I never writ, nor man ever lov'd.

William Shakespeare (1564–1616)

All love that has not friendship for its base
Is like a mansion built upon the sand.
Love, to endure life's sorrow and earth's woe,
needs friendship's solid mason-work below.

from *Wooings and Weddings in Many Climes*,
Louise Jordan Miln, 1900

The custom of celebrating wedding anniversaries is said to be of German origin. The traditional motifs for each year vary from country to country but the Silver, Golden and Diamond wedding anniversaries are always cause for celebration.

First	Paper
Second	Cotton
Third	Leather
Fourth	Silk, flowers or books
Fifth	Wood
Sixth	Iron or sugar

Seventh	Copper or wool
Eighth	Bronze
Ninth	Pottery
Tenth	Tin
Eleventh	Steel
Twelfth	Linen or silk
Thirteenth	Lace
Fourteenth	Ivory
Fifteenth	Crystal
Twentieth	China
Twenty-fifth	Silver
Thirtieth	Pearls
Thirty-fifth	Coral
Fortieth	Ruby
Forty-fifth	Sapphire
Fiftieth	Gold
Fifty-fifth	Emerald
Sixtieth	Diamond
Seventy-fifth	Diamond or platinum

The Golden Years

'Grow old along with me.'

———

All Kings, and all their favourites,
All glory of honours, beauties, wits,
The sun itself, which makes times, as they pass,
Is elder by a year now than it was
When thou and I first one another saw:
All other things to their destruction draw,
Only our love hath no decay;
This no tomorrow hath, nor yesterday,
Running it never runs from us away,
But truly keeps his first, last, everlasting day.

Two graves must hide thine and mine corse;
If one might, death were no divorce.
Alas, as well as other Princes, we
(Who Prince enough in one another be)
Must leave at last in death these eyes and ears,
Oft fed with true oaths, and with sweet salt tears;
But souls where nothing dwells but love
(All other thoughts being inmates) then shall prove
This, or a love increases there above,
When bodies to their graves, souls from their graves remove.

And then we shall be thoroughly blessed;
But we no more than all the rest.
Here upon the earth were Kings, and none but we
Can be such Kings, nor of subjects be;
Who is so safe as we? where none can do
Treason to us, except one of us two.

True and false fears let us refrain
Let us love nobly, and live and add again
Years and years unto years, till we attain
To write threescore: this is the second of our reign.

John Donne (1572–1631), 'The Anniversary'

To love a person means to agree to grow old with him.

Albert Camus

To My Dear and Loving Husband

If ever two were one, then surely we.
If ever man were loved by wife, then thee;
If ever wife was happy in a man,
Compare with me ye women if you can.
I prize thy love more than whole
  mines of gold,
Or all the riches that the East doth hold.
My love is such that rivers cannot quench,
Nor ought but love from thee, give
  recompence.
Thy love is such I can no way repay,
The heavens reward thee manifold I pray.
Then while we live, in love lets so persever,
That when we live no more, we may live ever.

Anne Bradstreet (1612–72)

'Thee, Mary, with this ring I wed,'
So, fourteen years ago, I said.
Behold another ring! 'For what?'
To wed thee o'er again — why not?

With that first ring I married youth,
Grace beauty, innocence, and truth;
Taste long admired, sense long revered,
And all my Molly then appeared,

If she by merit since disclosed,
Prove twice the woman I supposed,
I plead that double merit now,
To justify a double vow.

Here then, to-day, — with faith as sure,
With ardour as intense and pure,
As when amidst the rites divine
I took thy troth, and plighted mine, —
To thee sweet girl, my second ring,
A token, and a pledge, I bring;
With this I wed, till death us part,
Thy riper virtues to my heart:
Those virtues which, before untried,

The wife has added to the bride —
Those virtues, whose progressive claim,
Endearing wedlock's very name,
My soul enjoys, my song approves,
For conscience' sake as well as love's.

For why? — They show me every hour
Honour's high thought, affection's power,
Discretion's deed, sound judgment's sentence,
And teach me all things — but repentance.

Samuel Bishop (1731-95)

Grow old along with me!
The best is yet to be,
The last of life, for which the first was made:
Our times are in his hand
Who saith, 'A whole I planned,
Youth shows but half; trust God: see all, nor be afraid!'

Robert Browning (1812–89), from 'Rabbi Ben Ezra'

Love, let us live as we have lived, nor lose
    The little names that were the first night's grace,
And never come the day that sees us old,
    I still your lad, and you my little lass.

Let me be older than Nestor's years,
    And you the Sibyl, if we heed it not.
What should we know, we two, of ripe old age?
We'll have its richness, and the years forgot.

Ausonius (4th century AD), 'To His Wife'

Acknowledgements

Warm thanks are extended to the following people:

Litsa Moessis-Soulakellis
Litsa Flowers, McMahons Point, Sydney
for the flowers

Debbie Thornton
Deb's Designing Touch, Hurlstone Park, Sydney
for the page boy heart and flowergirl and guest baskets

Sweet Art
Paddington, Sydney
for the cake and sweets

Amoret Tanner
for the ephemera

Cheryl Hingley, Rosemary Loder, Bernice Martin,
Barbara Nixon, Gwen Page, Valerie Sadlier, Cathy Wadling
for providing props

And special thanks to Catherine Martin and Andrew Elton
for making this book such a pleasure to do.